Place-names of Leicestershire & Rutland

JILL BOURNE

LEICESTERSHIRE LIBRARIES & INFORMATION SERVICE

Leicestershire County Council
Libraries and Information Service 1977

SBN 85022 010 6

CONTENTS

Maps

Acknowledgements

The purpose of this book is to provide a complete and comprehensive guide to Leicestershire and Rutland place-names. All of the information has been gathered from the work of eminent scholars in the field of place-names studies and as such it is as accurate as it is possible to be at the time of publication.

The main sources of information I have used are:

The Concise Oxford Dictionary of English Place-Names — Eilert Ekwall. O.U.P. 4th Ed. 1960. This is a detailed and comprehensive work. Available in most public libraries.

English Place-Names — Kenneth Cameron. Batsford 1961. This is issued as a paper-back published by University Paper-backs Methuen & Co.

English Place-Name Elements — Vols. xxv and xxvi 1956 Cambridge University Press — The English Place-Name Society — A.H. Smith — 2nd Rev. Ed. 1971. These volumes can also be found in most public libraries.

The Origin of English Place Names — P.H. Reaney. Published by Routledge, Keegan Paul 1960. This is also obtainable from public libraries.

The only comprehensive study of Leicestershire and Rutland place-names is Dr. Barrie Cox's unpublished Ph. D. thesis. This is a very detailed work using every known early spelling of all the places in both counties. Every place-name in this publication has been checked against Dr. Cox's conclusions so that the reader can use the information with confidence. I am very grateful to Dr. Cox for allowing me to quote from his work. A copy of Dr. Cox's thesis is in the Leicestershire Collection at the Information Centre, Bishop Street, Leicester.

My thanks are due to the County Librarian; and especially to David Antill, Librarian, Publications and Public Relations, for his careful work in guiding this booklet through to publication.

Foreword

by G.H. MARTIN, Professor of History, University of Leicester

The place-names and names of the features of the English countryside are an ancient and continuous record of our history. Their study enlarges our knowledge not only of topography and human settlement, but of institutions and of our language itself. The decipherment of place-names is a highly technical matter, as Mrs. Bourne's references show, but her work is in the best sense an elementary one, which will introduce her readers to a wide range of expert knowledge. Those who take this book up to discover the origins of Croxton Kerrial or Tixover will find an answer to their question, and then beyond it the materials upon which the answer is based. If they choose to go further, they will open enquiries that will take them far into the resources of the Public Library and the national collections that stand behind it, and by those means they will discover worlds other than those of our familiar roads and signposts.

The examination of place-names however, depends not only on the general study of history and philology, but also on minute local enquiry and observation. The knowledge represented here is not something closed and settled, but is constantly augmented and developed. The reader who is drawn on from casual references to the systematic and considered investigation of his own locality may find himself making his own contribution to one of the most beguiling and satisfying historical studies.

The Place Names of Leicestershire and Rutland

In trying to find out what a place-name means there is no point in just guessing; even after careful analysis of early spellings the interpretation of a name is not always clear. Both the spelling and pronunciation have usually changed so much over the centuries that the modern form of the word may, at best, bear only a slight resemblance to the original form. The early forms of names are to be found in documents such as: The Anglo-Saxon Chronicle, Pipe Rolls, Charter Rolls, Assize Rolls, and many other documentary sources which vary from place to place. The earliest known spelling for most places comes from the Domesday Book – a survey made in 1086 – ordered by William the Conqueror, in order to assess the value of his lands in England. The scribes who compiled Domesday Book were Norman so the spelling is the result of their having to render unfamiliar sounds into their own language. Domesday entries for Leicester and Rutland are complete although a few settlements in Rutland are not listed separately but are joined with the rest of the lands of Edith, wife of Edward the Confessor.

Originally place-names were colloquial descriptions of settlements passed on by word of mouth, changing slightly from time to time until they became a word picture of a place. In some way every name is a description enabling the place to be readily identified. Hence through place-name study we are able to catch a glimpse of what particular parts of England may have looked like, and of some of the people who lived here a thousand or more years ago.

Most place-names fall broadly into two main groups: those which relate to the local topography and those which describe the settlement in some way. (Some names contain elements descriptive of both). Topographical names show some of the more important features of the landscape. For instance: the head of a valley – BITTESWELL, a stream – CLAYBROOKE, a ford – SHARNFORD, a spur of land – HOBY, the colour of the land – RATCLIFFE. Some names tell us about the vegetation at the time of the naming: ash trees – ASHBY, plum trees – PLUNGAR, willows – WITHCOTE. Animals occurring in large numbers account for other names: FOXTON, CRANOE, MOWSLEY, TIXOVER.

Habitative names most plainly reveal the settlement by different invaders. The earliest names are those which were taken over by the Anglo-Saxons from the Britons, and it is possible that the British might have taken over existing names from their predecessors as they were not the first inhabitants. The Romans for example are remembered by LEICESTER (Ratae) and CASTERTON; from the mid fifth century onwards England was invaded and settled by Germanic tribes of

ANGLES, SAXONS and JUTES. The area of Leicestershire and Rutland was a part of the regions which were settled by a number of peoples known collectively as the Middle-Angles. The invasion would have been slow but the conquest of England would have been complete by the end of the seventh century. Anglo-Saxon place-names cover the period from the fifth to eleventh centuries; linguistically this period is called Old English. Only some of these Anglo-Saxon names can be identified as belonging definitely to the period before the ninth century such as names ending with the element *—ham, —ingaham,* and *—ingas.* The exact chronology of these names is still a matter of some debate. I would recommend any reader who wishes to explore this area in more detail to read **Place-Name Evidence for the Anglo-Saxon Invasion and Scandinavian Settlements,** edited by Kenneth Cameron & C.M. Gelling and published by the English Place-Name Society, 1976. Other elements such as *tun,, cot, wick,* and *worth,* seems to occur throughout the whole period of Anglo-Saxon settlement.

Names of Scandinavian origin appear during the late ninth, tenth and eleventh centuries, the time of the Viking settlements. The Vikings were Norwegians and Danes. The Danes settled in the East Midlands and part of Yorkshire whilst the Norwegians, who mostly came by way of Ireland, settled in the Lake District, Cheshire, Lancashire and North Yorkshire. The languages of the settlers were different from Old English but had many similarities. The Vikings gradually adopted the language of the Anglo-Saxons whilst at the same time introducing new words. The most distinctive Scandinavian imported elements are *—by* and *—thorp.* The Scandinavian influence is particularly noticeable in Leicestershire and Rutland as both Counties were part of the Danelaw.

Those names which post-date the Norman conquest are usually the names of manorial lords added on to an earlier name, for example DUNTON BASSETT, MELTON MOWBRAY, ASHBY DE LA ZOUCH. But in the main, by far the vast majority of English place-names were in existence by the time of William the Conqueror.

Deserted Villages (see map on page 5)

The Black Death struck the country in 1348. Over thirty years, successive outbreaks of the plague reduced the population by at least one third: this had profound consequences on the whole way of life, and in some areas changed the appearance of the landscape.

There are at least 1,300 deserted village sites in England. Most of these abandoned settlements are in the Midlands and eastern England. In many instances the Black Death as such was not the immediate cause of a settlement being abandoned. Villages which had been settled late, often on less productive land, would have already been struggling. Desertion would have been gradual, with successive generations finding survival difficult with the plague rendering their task finally impossible.

This was the time of the development of the wool trade and the ultimate abandonment of a settlement was often brought about by landlords who had difficulty in finding labour to work arable land and so wanted to enclose the open arable fields to use the land for pasture. There are many instances of landlords evicting tenants and demolishing their mud-walled dwellings; leaving the peasants to go away to make whatever life they could.

Often the only evidence that there ever was a community on the site of a deserted village, are the grass-covered banks where the houses once stood and the hollows where once there were lanes.

In the County are three deserted settlements which have not yet been found. Their names appear in Domesday and never occur again. They are LILINGE, NETONE and PLOTELEI with a population of 14, 10 and 7 (adults) respectively. Small numbers, but no smaller than countless other settlements which survived, flourished and are alive today.

The desertion and extinction of settlements has been researched by many scholars, the most eminent being Maurice Berresford, his books are brilliant studies of this subject.

1 Maurice Berresford — **The Lost Villages of England** Lutterworth Press 1954

2 M. Berresford and J.G. Hurst — **Deserted Mediaeval Villages** Lutterworth Press 1971

A publication on the lost villages of Leicestershire and Rutland is being prepared by this author.

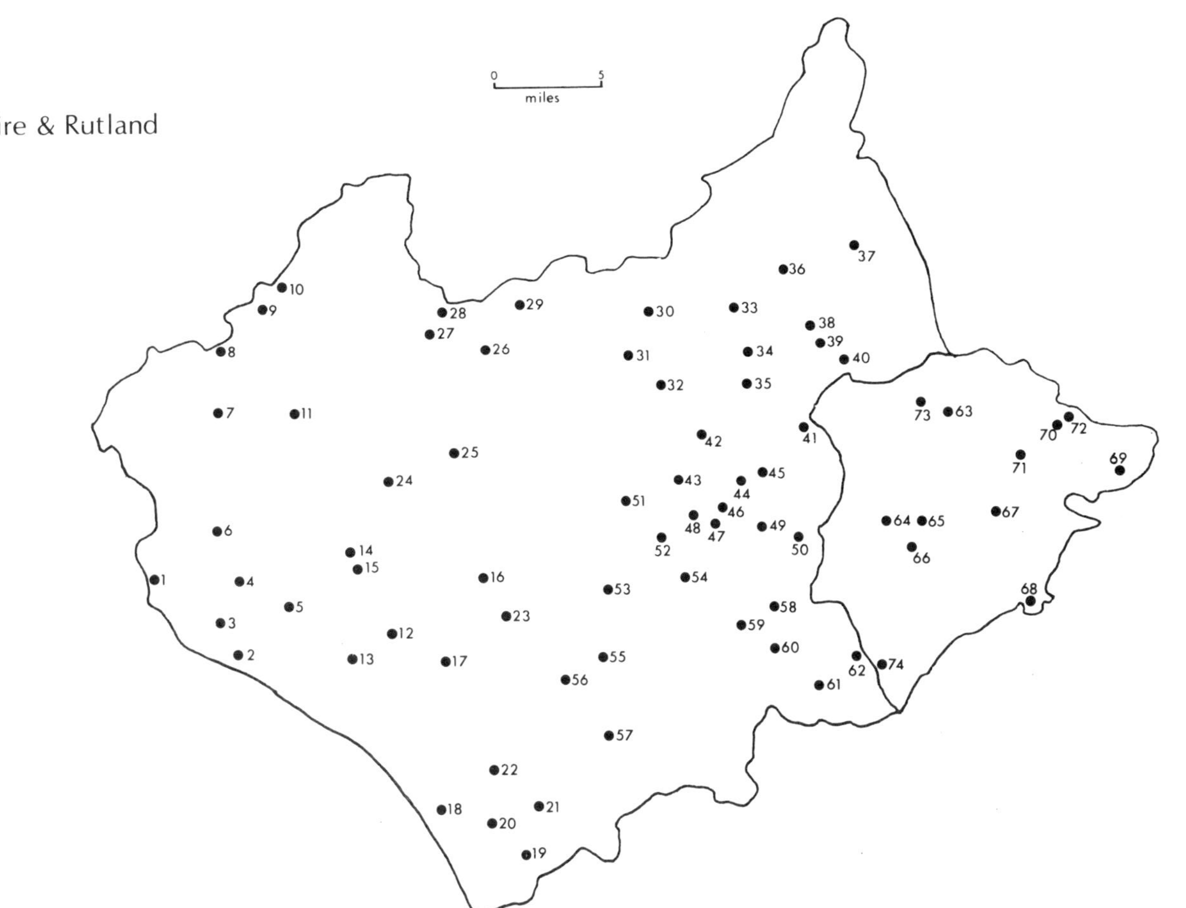

Sites of Deserted Medieval Villages

Deserted Villages

LEICESTERSHIRE

1. Weston
2. Lindley
3. Atherton
4. Wellsborough
5. Ambion
6. Gopsall
7. Willesley
8. Woodcote
9. Staunton Harold
10. Andreskirk
11. Alton
12. Normanton Turville
13. Elmesthorpe
14. Naneby
15. Brascote
16. Lubbesthorpe
17. Potters Marston
18. Bittesby
19. Stormsworth
20. Misterton
21. Poultney
22. Cotes de Val
23. Aldeby
24. Whittington
25. Bradgate
26. Shelthorpe
27. Garendon
28. Dishley
29. Prestwold
30. Shoby
31. Willowes
32. Brooksby
33. Welby
34. Sysonby
35. Eye Kettleby
36. Ringolthorp
37. Bescaby
38. Brentingby
39. Wyfordby
40. Stapleford
41. Leesthorpe
42. Newbold Folville
43. Baggrave
44. North Marefield
45. Newbold Saucy
46. Lowesby
47. Cold Newton
48. Quenby
49. Whatborough
50. Withcote
51. Hamilton
52. Ingarsby
53. Stretton Magna
54. Frisby
55. Wistow
56. Foston
57. Knaptoft
58. Keythorpe
59. Noseley
60. Othorpe
61. Prestgrave
62. Holyoaks

RUTLAND

63. Alstoe
64. Brooke
65. Gunthorpe
66. Martinsthorpe
67. Normanton
68. Tixover
69. Folethorpe
70. Hardwick
71. Horn
72. Pickworth
73. Wenton
74. Snelston

Elements used in Leicestershire and Rutland Place Names

The following list includes most of the elements (other than personal names) that are found in the county.

The abbreviations are:

O.E.	Old English
O.N.	Old Norse
O.D.	Old Danish
O.Fr.	Old French
Latin	

O.E.	*aeppel*	=	'apple, fruit in general.' **Appleby**
O.E.	*aesc*	=	'an ash tree.' **Ashwell**
O.E.	*anstiga*	=	'a path for one, a narrow footpath.' **Anstey**
O.E.	*baerlic*	=	'barley.' **Barleythorpe**
O.E.	*bar*	=	'a boar.' **Barwell**
O.E.	*bearu*	=	'a wood, a grove'. **Barrow**
O.E.	*bece*	=	'a stream, a valley.' **Cotesbach**
O.E.	*bel*	=	'a space or interval or a beacon or funeral pyre.' **Belton**
O.E.	*beo*	=	'bee.' **Beeby**
O.E.	*beorg*	=	'a hill, a mound.' **Barrowden**
O.E.	*blaec*	=	'black, dark-coloured, dark.' **Blackfordby**
O.E.	*botl*	=	'a dwelling, a house.' **Bottesford**
O.E.	*brad*	=	'broad, spacious.' **Bradgate**
O.E.	*broc*	=	'a brook, a stream.' **Brooke**
O.E.	*burh*	=	'a fortified place.' **Burley**
O.E.	*burna*	=	'a stream, a spring.' **Medbourne**
O.N.	*by*	=	'a farmstead, a village.' **Ashby**
O.E.	*bytme*	=	'the head of a valley.' **Bitteswell**
O.E.	*cald*	=	'cold, bleak, exposed.' **Caldecott, Langton Caudle**
O.E.	*ceaster*	=	'a city, an old fortification, a Roman Town.' **Leicester**
O.E.	*ceorl*	=	'a churl, one of the lower classes of freemen, an ordinary freeman, a peasant.' **Carlton**
O.E.	*cild*	=	'a child, a young person.' **Chilcote**
O.E.	*claeg*	=	'clay, clayey soil.' **Claybrooke**
O.E.	*claen*	=	'clean, clear of weeds.' **Glenfield**
O.E.	*clif*	=	'a cliff, a bank.' **Ratcliffe**
O.E.	*cniht*	=	'a youth, a servant, a soldier.' **Knighton**
O.E.	*col*	=	'coal (especially charcoal).' This element is difficult to separate from 'col' meaning cool. **Coleorton**
O.E.	*cot*	=	'a cottage, a hut, a shelter, a den.' **Kimcote**
O.E.	*craeft*	=	'a machine, an engine.' **Croft**

O.E. *crawe* = 'a crow'. **Cranoe**
O.E. *croft* = 'a small enclosed field.' **Ulverscroft**
O.E. *cros* = 'a cross'. **Twycross**
O.E. *cwen* = 'a queen'. **Quenby**
O.E. *cweorn* = 'a quern, a handmill.' **Quorndon**
O.E. *dael* = 'a valley.' **Ragdale**
O.E. *denu* = 'a valley.' **Whissendine**
O.E. *draeg* = 'a drag, a portage, a slip-way, a dray.' **Drayton**
O.E. *dryge* = 'dry, dried up.' **Stoke Dry**
O.E. *dun* = 'a hill'. **Barrowden**
O.E. *ea* = 'a river, a stream.' **Ketton**
O.E. *east* = 'eastern, east.' **Eastwell**
O.E. *efes* = 'eaves, edge of wood.' **Woodhouse Eaves**
O.E. *eg* = 'an island.' **Sheepy**
O.E. *faesten* = 'a stronghold.' **Stockerston**
O.E. *feld* = 'open country.' **Glenfield, Highfields**
O.E. *ford* = 'ford, a shallow place across a stream.' **Desford**
O.E. *fox* = 'fox.' **Foxton**
O.E. *Frisa* = 'a Frisian, a native of Friesland.' **Frisby**
O.E. *fyrhth* = 'a wood, woodland.' **Braunstone Frith**
O.N. *gata* = 'a road or a street.' **Gartree Road**
O.E. *geat* = 'an opening, a gap.' **Bradgate**
O.E. *gop* = 'a slave, a servant.' **Gopsall**
O.Fr. *grange* = 'an outlying farm belonging to a religious house.' **Knighton Grange**
O.E. *greot* = 'gravel.' **Greetham**
O.E. *grof* = 'a stream, the hollow which a stream makes, a pit.' **Groby**
O.E. *gylden* = 'golden.' **Gilmorton**
O.E. *haeth* = 'a heath, heather.' **Donnington-le-Heath**
O.E. *hald* = 'a shelter, refuge, a stronghold.' **Halstead**
O.E. *halh* = 'a nook, a corner of land, a water meadow.' **Ryhall**
O.E. *ham* = 'a village, a village community, a homestead.' **Clipsham**
O.E. *hamol* = 'maimed, mutilated, flat-topped.' **Hambleton**
O.E. *heah* = high'. **Higham**
O.N. *heithr* = 'heath, uncultivated land.' **Heather**
O.E. *hlyde* = 'a noisy stream.' **Lyddington**
O.E. *hoh* = 'a heel, a spur of land.' **Hoby**
O.E. *holt* = 'a wood, a thicket.' **Holt**
O.E. *hungor* = 'hunger, famine.' **Hungarton**
O.E. *hwaete* = 'wheat.' **Whatborough**
O.E. *hwit* = 'white.' **Whitwell**
O.E. *hyll* = 'a hill.' **Gopsall**
O.E. hyrst = 'a hillock, a copse.' **Bringhurst**
O.E. *ing* = 'connective word linking a first element — a personal name or a significant word — to a final element. **Donnington**
O.E. *ingas* = 'a plural element used in compounded place-names denoting groups of people.' **Skeffington**
O.N. *kirkju-by* = 'a village with a church.' **Kirby**

O.E. *land*	=	'land.' **Rutland**
O.E. *lane*	=	'a lane, a narrow road.'
O.E. *lang*	=	'long.' **Langham**
O.Fr. *launde*	=	'an open space in woodland.' **Launde**
O.E. *leah*	=	'a wood, a clearing in a wood.' **Wardley**
O.E. *lind*	=	'a lime-tree.' **Lyndon**
O.E. *linden*	=	'growing with lime-trees.' **Linford**
O.E. *lytel*	=	'little, small.' **Littlethorpe**
O.E. *maed*	=	'meadow.' **Medbourne**
Latin *magna*	=	'great.' **Ashby Magna**
O.Fr. *market*	=	'market'. **Market Overton**
O.E. *Merce*	=	'the Mercians':(The English tribe which settled in the West Midlands). **Markfield**
O.E. *mersc*	=	'watery land, a marsh.' **Marston**
O.E. *middel*	=	'middle.' **Melton**
O.Fr. *mont*	=	'a mount, a hill.' **Mountsorrel**
O.E. *mor*	=	'a moor, barren waste-land.' **Morcott**
O.E. *meos* or *mos*	=	'a marsh, a bog.' **Catmose**
O.E. *mus*	=	'a mouse.' **Mowsley**
O.E. *myln*	=	'a mill.'
O.E. *mynster*	=	'a monastery, a church served by secular clergy.' **Misterton**
O.E. *neothera*	=	'lower.' **Netherfield**
O.E. *niew*	=	'new.' **Newarke**
O.E. *north*	=	'northern, north.' **North Luffenham**
O.E. *ofer*	=	'slope, hill, ridge.' **Overton**
O.E. *ora*	=	'a border, a margin, a bank.' **Overton** The two elements are often interchangeable)
O.E. *oxa*	=	'an ox.' **Exton**
O.E. *preast*	=	'a priest.' **Preston**
Latin *parva*	=	'small.' **Glen Parva**
O.E. *read*	=	'red.' **Ratcliffe**
O.E. *risc*	=	'a rush'. **Rushall**
O.E. *ryge*	=	'rye.' **Ryhall**
O.E. *sceap*	=	'a sheep.' **Shepshed**
O.E. *scelf*	=	'a rock, a ledge.' **Earl Shilton**
O.E. *smith*	=	'a smith, a worker on metal.' **Smeeton Westerby**
O.E. *staca*	=	'a stake.' **Stathern**
O.E. *stan*	=	'a stone or rock.' **Humberstone**
O.E. *stapol*	=	'a post, a pillar.' **Stapleford**
O.E. *stede*	=	'a place.' **Halstead**
O.E. *stoc*	=	'a place, a secondary settlement.' **Stoughton**
O.E. *stocc*	=	'a tree-trunk, a log of wood.' **Stockerston**
O.E. *straet*	=	'a Roman road.' **Stretton**
O.N. *switha*	=	'land cleared by burning.' **Swithland**
O.E. *suth*	=	'south, southern.' **South Luffenham**
O.E. *teag*	=	'a small enclosure.' **Teigh**
O.E. *ticcen*	=	'a kid, a young goat.' **Tixover**
O.E. *thorn*	=	'thorn.' **Thornton**

O.D. *thorp* = 'a secondary settlement, a dependent outlying farmstead.' **Bruntingthorpe**

O.E. *thyrne* = 'thorn-bush.' **Stathern**

O.N.

O.D. *toft* = 'an enclosure, a building plot.' **Scraptoft**

O.E. *tun* = 'an enclosure, a farmstead, a village.' **Stockerston**

O.E. *uferra* = 'higher, upper.' **Orton**

O.E. *up* = 'up, higher up, upon.' **Uppingham**

O.N. *vikingr* = 'a roving pirate, a viking.' **Wigston Magna**

O.E. *waeter* = 'water.' **Willoughby Waterless**

O.E. *wald* = 'woodland, high forest land, wold.' **Waltham**

O.E. *walh* = 'a foreigner, a Welshman, a serf.' **Walcote**

O.E. *weard* = 'watch, ward, protection.' **Wardley**

O.E. *wella* = 'a well, a spring, a stream.' **Ashwell**

O.E. *west* = 'west, western.' **Weston**

O.E. *wic* = 'a dwelling, a farm, a dairy farm.' **Whitwick**

O.E. *withig* = 'a willow.' **Withcote**

O.E. *worth* = 'an enclosure.' **Pickworth**

O.E. *wudu* = 'a wood, a grove, a forest.' **Charnwood**

O.E. *yppe* = 'a raised place, a hill.' **Uppingham**

An Alphabetical List of the Place Names of Leicestershire and Rutland

1. The places are arranged alphabetically. Leicestershire and Rutland are listed separately. All of the places are to be found on the 1 inch to the mile Ordnance Survey maps. Deserted settlements are not listed, they are marked on the map on Page 5.

2. Numbers in the first column refer to the grid map between Pages 14 & 15.

   Every place has been given a map reference but the name may not necessarily be printed on the map. These references are indicated thus: ***F9**

3. The Second column gives the modern spelling of the name of the settlement.

4. The third column gives the earliest recorded spelling and the spelling given in Domesday Book. (D.B.) (In most instances this is the first recorded spelling). In those cases where the first recorded spelling is other than Domesday I have given the exact reference.

5. The fourth column shows the elements of the names (and their meaning). Where there is any significant difference of opinion between Ekwall and Dr. Barrie Cox I have made a note of it. To show these differences I have used the abbreviations Ek. and B.C.

6. On Page 7 there is a complete list of all the elements found in Leicestershire and Rutland place names. These examples show that it is seldom possible to recognise the various elements from the modern spelling. In order to disentangle the elements it is essential to consider all the early spellings.

   The abbreviations are:

O.E.	Old English
O.N.	Old Norse
O.D.	Old Danish
O.Fr.	Old French

Leicestershire

C/D9	Ab Kettleby	Chetelbi — DB	Ketil's *by* (village or homestead)
H10	Allexton	Adelachestone — DB	Eadlac's *tun* (settlement)
F6	Anstey	Anstige — DB	O.E. *anstiga* — (a narrow footpath) probably one going up a hill.
F2	Appleby Magna	Aplebi — DB	O.E. *aeppel* — (apple tree) *by* — (village or farmstead).
F2	Appleby Parva	Aplebi — DB	O.E. *aeppel* — (apple) tree *by* — (village or farmstead).
I7	Arnesby	Erendesbi — DB	Iarand's *by* (village or farmstead).
D8/9	Asfordby	Osferdebie — DB	Asford's *by* (village or farmstead).
E2/3	Ashby-de-la-Zouch	Ascebi — DB	*By* (village or farmstead) where the ash trees grew. Zouch is a family name from the french Souche — stump.
***F/9**	Ashby Folville	Ascbi — DB	*By* (village or farmstead) where the ash trees grew. Named from one of the Follevilles in France, one is in Calvados in Normandy.
I6	Ashby Magna	Essebi — DB	*By* (village or farmstead) where the ash trees grew.
J5/6	Ashby Parva	Essebi — DB	*By* (village or farmstead) where the ash trees grew.
I4/5	Aston Flamville	Eston — Episcopal Registers	O.E. *east tun* (settlement)
G/6	Aylestone	Ailestone — DB	AEgel's *tun* (settlement)
***F9**	Baggrave	Badegraye — DB	O.E. Babba's *graf* (grove). This is a woman's name.
F4/5	Bagworth	Bageworde — DB	Bacga's *worth* (enclosure).
F7/8	Barkby	Barchebi — DB	Bark's *by* (village or farmstead). The outlying farmstead of Barkby.
F7/8	Barkby Thorpe		The outlying farmstead of Barkby.
B10	Barkestone	Barchestone — DB	Bark's *tun* (settlement).
F/G4	Barlestone	Berulvestone — DB	Berwulf's or Beornwulf's *tun* (settlement).
D/E6	Barrow-upon-Soar	Barhou — DB	O.E. *bearu* — (a grove or wood).
***F8**	Barsby	Barnesbi — DB	*Barn's* (child) *by* (village or settlement.) Barn — child occurs as a by-name and as a fictitious Christian name.

***F4**	Barton-in-the-Beans	Bartone – DB	O.E. *bere* (barley, corn) *tun* (settlement). The barley or corn farm.
***H5**	Barwell	Barwalle – 1043 Diplomatarium Anglicum Barewelle – DB	O.E. *bar* (boar) *wella* (stream)
***E5**	Beaumanor Park	Beumaner 1265 – Charter Rolls	O.F. *Beau* (beautiful) *maner* (seat).
F8	Beeby	Bebi – DB	*By* (village or farmstead) where the bees were kept). Could mean bee village.
G7	Belgrave	Merdegrave – DB	The DB name is probably *merde* (martin's) *graf* (grove). After the conquest the first element seems to have become associated with the Old French – *merde* meaning excrement or filth and by 1135 had been replaced by *bel* meaning beautiful.
G10	Belton	Beltona 1125 – The Leicestershire Survey	*Bel* might be O.N. *bael* meaning a point of time or interval, interspace. If so then the word might well have been used of a glade in a forest or a *tun* (settlement) on dry ground in fenny country. Bel can also mean a beacon or funeral pyre.
B10/11	Belvoir	Belveder 1130 – Pipe Rolls.	O.F. *Bel* (beautiful) *vedeir* (view).
***C10**	Bescaby	Bersaltebi 1194 – Pipe Rolls	Ekwall suggests that the meaning of this name is Saltby with the O.E. *beorg* (hill), thus Hill Salty. Bescaby is 1½ miles away from the place known today as Saltby and higher up the hill. Cox suggests that this is a personal name – Bergskald's *by* (village or farmstead).
G9	Billesdon	Billesdone – DB	The *dun* (hill) and the *leah* (a clearirg in a wood) belonging to Bill which is a short form of Bilheard. Cox thinks that it is probably Bil's hill. Bill may also mean a hill or promontary.
F7	Birstall	Burstelle – DB	O.E. *burg-steall* – in the sense of a city. Here it means the site of a burg i.e. old disused fort.
J5	Bittesby	Bichesbie – DB	Byttel's *by* (village or farmstead).
J5/6	Bitteswell	Betmeswelle	O.E. *bytme* (head of a valley) plus *wella* (well or spring). 'The stream or spring in the head of a valley'.
H6	Blaby	Bladi – DB	Blar's *by* (village or farmstead).

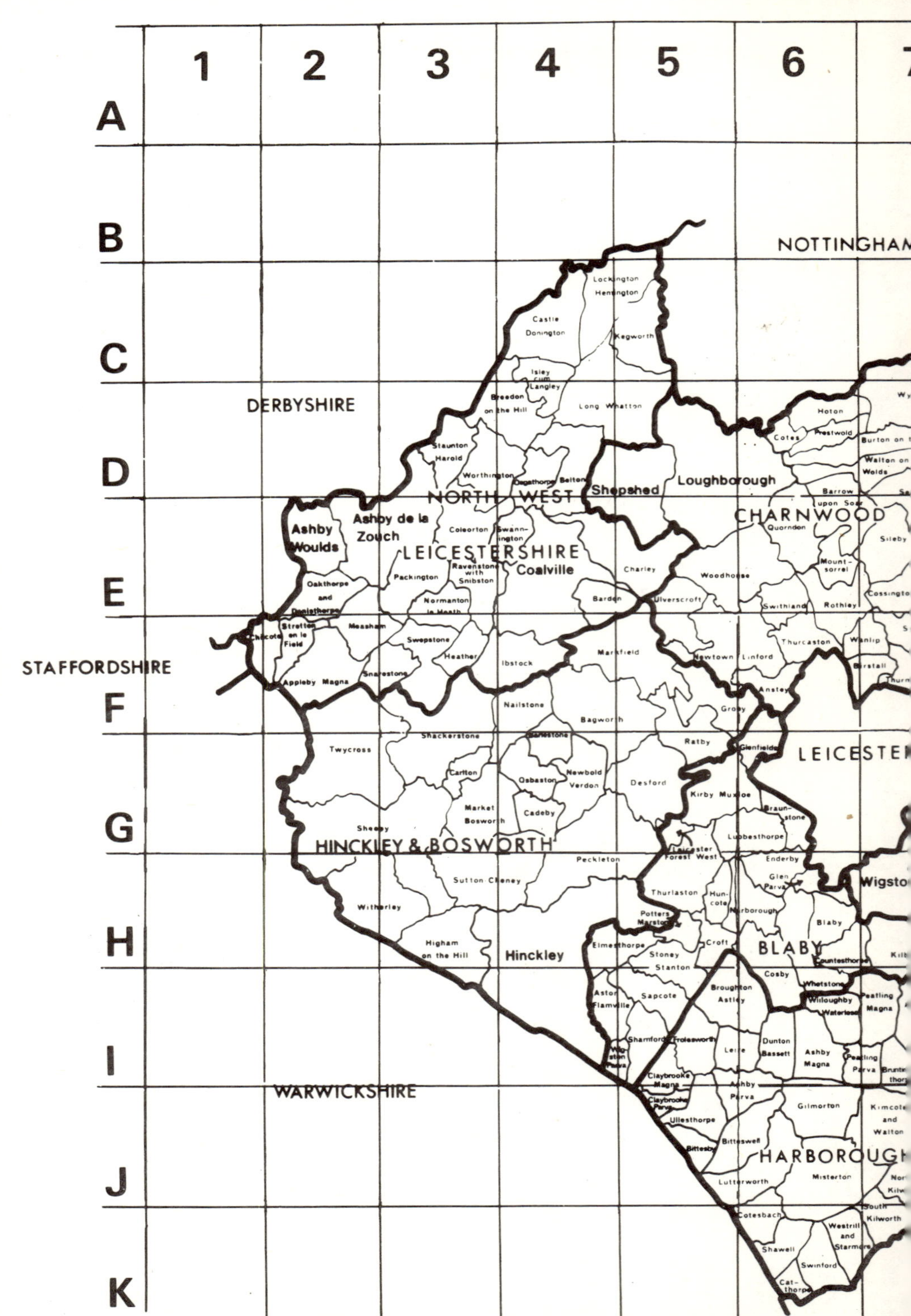
1
2
3
4
5
6
A
B
C
D
E
F
G
H
I
J
K
NOTTINGHAM
DERBYSHIRE
STAFFORDSHIRE
WARWICKSHIRE
NORTH WEST LEICESTERSHIRE
CHARNWOOD
LEICESTER
HINCKLEY & BOSWORTH
BLABY
HARBOROUGH
Castle Donington
Kegworth
Long Whatton
Breedon on the Hill
Staunton Harold
Worthington
Belton
Shepshed
Loughborough
Ashby Woulds
Ashby de la Zouch
Coleorton
Coalville
Packington
Normanton le Heath
Oakthorpe and Donisthorpe
Measham
Chilcote
Stretton en le Field
Appleby Magna
Snarestone
Swepstone
Heather
Ibstock
Markfield
Charley
Bardon
Ulverscroft
Woodhouse
Quorndon
Hoton
Cotes
Prestwold
Barrow upon Soar
Mountsorrel
Sileby
Swithland
Rothley
Thurcaston
Wanlip
Birstall
Newtown Linford
Anstey
Groby
Ratby
Glenfields
Nailstone
Bagworth
Shackerstone
Twycross
Carlton
Osbaston
Newbold Verdon
Desford
Kirby Muxloe
Braunstone
Market Bosworth
Cadeby
Sheepy
Peckleton
Sutton Cheney
Witherley
Higham on the Hill
Hinckley
Lubbesthorpe
Leicester Forest West
Enderby
Glen Parva
Wigston
Thurlaston
Huncote
Narborough
Blaby
Potters Marston
Elmesthorpe
Stoney Stanton
Croft
Countesthorpe
Cosby
Whetstone
Willoughby Waterleys
Peatling Magna
Aston Flamville
Sapcote
Broughton Astley
Sharnford
Frolesworth
Leire
Dunton Bassett
Ashby Magna
Peatling Parva
Claybrooke Magna
Claybrooke Parva
Ashby Parva
Gilmorton
Ullesthorpe
Bittesby
Bitteswell
Lutterworth
Misterton
Cotesbach
Shawell
Westrill and Starmore
Swinford
South Kilworth
Catthorpe

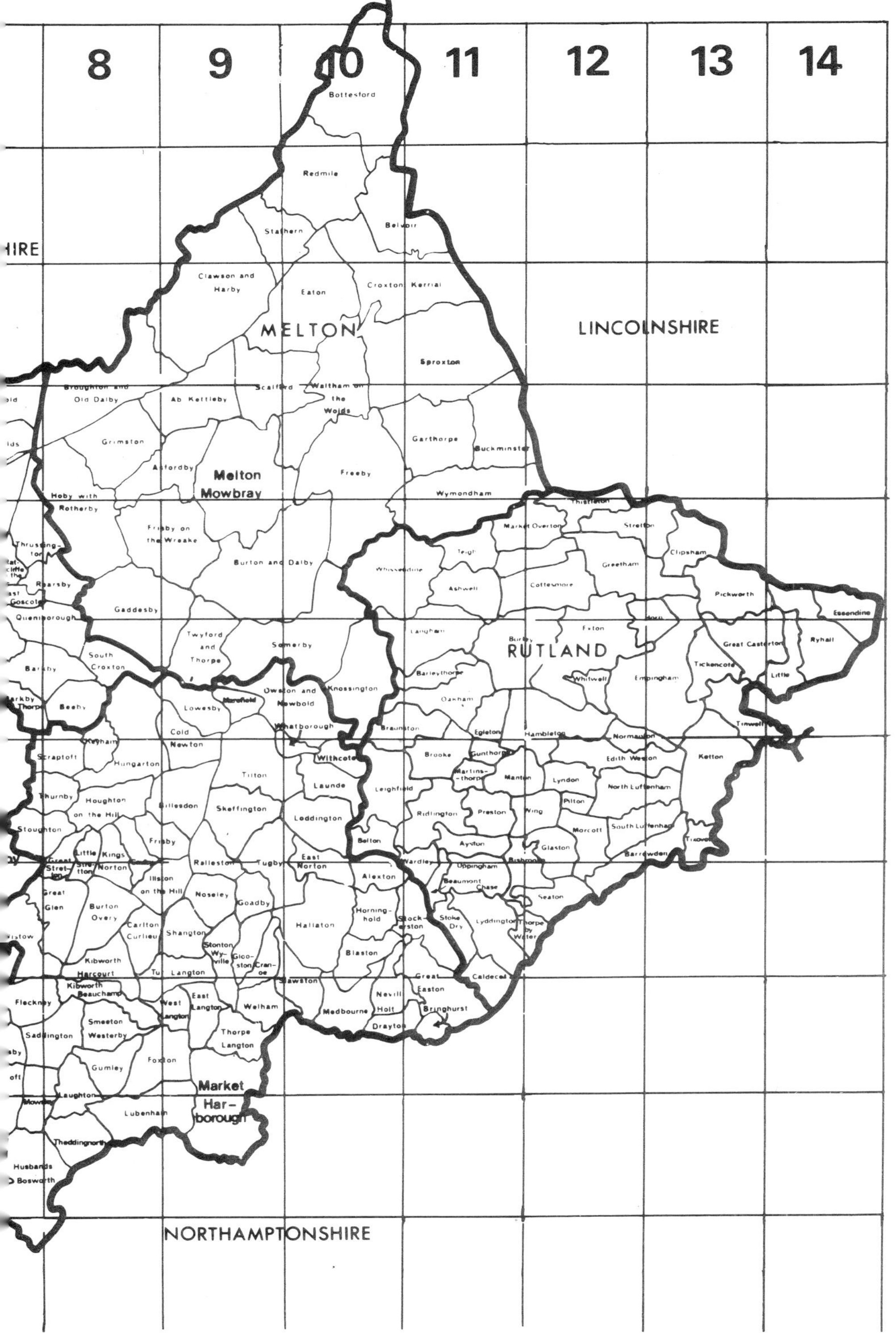

8
9
10
11
12
13
14
Bottesford
Redmile
Belvoir
Stathern
Clawson and Harby
Eaton
Croxton Kerrial
MELTON
LINCOLNSHIRE
Sproxton
Broughton and Old Dalby
Ab Kettleby
Scalford
Waltham on the Wolds
Grimston
Garthorpe
Buckminster
Asfordby
Melton Mowbray
Freeby
Wymondham
Hoby with Rotherby
Frisby on the Wreake
Thistleton
Market Overton
Stretton
Teigh
Clipsham
Whissendine
Burton and Dalby
Greetham
Ashwell
Cottesmore
Pickworth
Rearsby
Gaddesby
Essendine
Queniborough
Twyford and Thorpe
Somerby
Langham
Exton
Burley
RUTLAND
Great Casterton
Ryhall
South Croxton
Barsby
Barleythorpe
Whitwell
Empingham
Tickencote
Little
Owston and Newbold
Knossington
Lowesby
Marefield
Beeby
Oakham
Whatborough
Braunston
Egleton
Hambleton
Normanton
Tinwell
Cold Newton
Keyham
Scraptoft
Hungarton
Withcote
Brooke
Gunthorpe
Edith Weston
Ketton
Tilton
Martinsthorpe
Manton
Lyndon
Launde
Leighfield
North Luffenham
Thurnby
Houghton on the Hill
Billesdon
Skeffington
Loddington
Ridlington
Preston
Wing
Pilton
Stoughton
Morcott
South Luffenham
Frisby
Belton
Ayston
Glaston
Tixover
Little Stretton
Kings Norton
Great Stretton
Rolleston
Tugby
East Norton
Wardley
Uppingham
Bisbrooke
Barrowden
Alexton
Illston on the Hill
Great Glen
Beaumont Chase
Noseley
Goadby
Seaton
Burton Overy
Horninghold
Stockerston
Stoke Dry
Lyddington
Thorpe by Water
Carlton Curlieu
Shangton
Hallaton
Stonton Wyville
Glooston
Cranoe
Blaston
Kibworth Harcourt
Tur Langton
Caldecott
Great Easton
Slawston
Kibworth Beauchamp
Fleckney
East Langton
West Langton
Welham
Nevill Holt
Medbourne
Bringhurst
Drayton
Smeeton Westerby
Saddington
Thorpe Langton
Foxton
Gumley
Market Harborough
Laughton
Lubenham
Theddingworth
Husbands Bosworth
NORTHAMPTONSHIRE

E2	Blackfordby	Blakefordebi – c. 1125 Leicestershire Survey	'The *by* (village or farmstead) at the black ford. As this village is in a coal area the water might well be blackened.
H10	Blaston	Bladestone – DB	Bleat's *tun* (settlement).
A10	Bottesford	Botesford – DB	The *ford* at the *botl* (house or dwelling place).
***F6**	Bradgate	Bradgate 1275 – Catalogue of Ancient Deeds	The *brad* (broad) *gata* (gap). (The way through or between the hills).
***C10**	Branston	Brantestone – DB	Brant's *tun* (settlement).
G6	Braunstone	Brantestone – DB	Brant's *tun* (settlement).
D4	Breedon-on-the-Hill	Briudun – c. 730 Bede	British hill name identical to the welsh *bre* plus the O.E. *dun* (hill).
***D9**	Brentingby	Brantingbia – c. 1125 Leicestershire Survey	Brant's *by* (village or farmstead).
I11	Bringhurst	Brunünghyrst 1188 – Charter Rolls	The *hyrst* (a hillock or copse) of Bryni's people.
***E8**	Brooksby	Brochesbi – DB	The *by* (village or farmstead) on the *broc* (brook) (Wreake).
I5/6	Broughton Astley	Brohtone – DB	*Tun* (settlement) on a *broc* (brook). Held by Thomas de Estleg in 1203.
I7	Bruntingthorpe	Brandinestor – DB	Branting's *thorp* (farm).
D11	Buckminster	Bucheminstre – DB	Bucca's minster or church.
***I4**	Burbage	Burhbeca 1043 D.A. Burbece – DB	Ek: O.E. *baec,* (hill, ridge) plus *burgh* (fortified place). The place is on the slope of a hill and B.C. suggests that the name means the brook or valley by the burg.
***F9**	Burrough-on-the-Hill	Burg – DB	The *burh* (fort) with earth ramparts. Fine Iron Age hill-fort.
***E9**	Burton Lazars	Burtone – DB	The *tun* (settlement) near the *burg* (old fortifications). The hospital of St. Lazarus for lepers was founded in 1135.
E9	Burton-in-the-Wolds	Burtone – DB	*Tun* (settlement) by a *burg* (old fortifications).
H8	Burton Overy	Burtone – DB	*Tun* (settlement) near an old fortification burg. Held by Robert de Novereia in 1229.
***G7**	Bushby	Buszebia 1175	Butr's *by* (village or farmstead).
G4	Cadeby	Catebi – DB	Kati's *by* (village or farmstead).
G3	Carlton	Karletone – 1209 Episcopal Registers	The *tun* (settlement) of the freemen or peasants.

H8	Carlton Curlieu	Carleton — DB	The *tun* (settlement) of the *Ceorl,* O.E. (freeman or peasants). This village was held by Robert de Curly in 13th cent; may be from Cully in Normandy.
C4	Castle Donington	Dunitone — DB	The *tun* (settlement) of Dunn's people.
K6	Catthorpe	Torp — DB	*Thorp,* the outlying farmstead. Cat is the name of an early owner.
*D10	Chadwell	Caldeuuelle — DB	*Cald* (cold) *wella* (stream).
F1/2	Chilcote	Cildecote — DB	O.E. *cilda cot* — literally children's cottage(s) but it is unlikely that this is the exact meaning. Both Cameron and Cox suggest that cot of the youngest son is the most likely.
*I9	Church Langton	Langetone — DB	O.E. *langa* (long) *tun* (settlement). First reference to Church Langton is in 1384.
I5	Claybrooke	Claibroc — DB	The *broc* (brook) with a *claeg* (clay) bed.
E4	Coalville		A late name. The town is in the coal district. The parish was formed in 1892.
F/G9	Cold Newton	Neutun — 1236 — The Book of Fees	The new *tun* (settlement), *cald* (cold, bleak, exposed).
*F10	Cold Overton	Ovretone — DB	O.E. Ulfera's *tun* (settlement), *cald* (cold, bleak, exposed).
E3	Coleorton		The *tun* (settlement) on the hill or ridge.
*G3	Congerstone	Cuningestone — DB	The King's *tun* (settlement).
F5	Copt Oak		Pollarded oak.
H/I6	Cosby	Cossibi — DB	Cossa's *by* (village or homestead).
E7	Cossington	Cosintone — DB	The *tun* (settlement) of Cusa's people.
*D10	Coston	Castone — DB	Katr's *tun* (settlement).
D6	Cotes	Cotes 1200 — Danelaw Charters	*Cotts* (cottages or shelters for animals, especially sheep).
*I6	Cotes de Val	Toniscote — DB	Tone's *cote* (cottage) later just: the cottages. Deville from the family of that name, perhaps from Normandy.
*K6	Cotesbach	Cotesbece — DB	Cote's *bece* (a stream, valley).
H6	Countesthorpe	Torp — 1209-35 Episcopal Registers	Thorp (farm). The Countess's farm.

H9	Cranoe	Craweho — DB	O.E. *crawena hoh*. (A headland frequented by crows).
H5	Croft	Crebre — DB	O.E. *craeft* (a machine or an engine). This may refer to a windmill or a watermill.
C10/11	Croxton Kerrial	Crontone — DB	Croc's *tun* (settlement). Granted to Bertram de Cryoil in 1242. The family name was taken from Criel in Seine in France.
***H3**	Dadlington	Dadelintona c 1190 Danelaw Charters	Daedela's tun. The first element is derived from an unrecorded personal name. *Tun* (settlement).
G5	Desford	Diresford — DB	Deor's *ford*.
C4	Diseworth	Diwort — DB	Digoth's *worth* (enclosure).
***D5**	Dishley	Dislea — DB	Digoth's *leah* (a clearing in a wood). Dishley is only four miles from Diseworth.
***E4**	Donnington-le-Heath	Duntone — DB	The *tun* (settlement) of Dun's people.
***E2**	Donisthorpe	Durandestorp — DB	Durand's *thorp* (farmstead).
I6	Dunton Basset	Doniton — DB	*Tun* (settlement) on a *dun* (hill). Held by Ralph Bassett in 1242.
***H5**	Earl Shilton	Sceltone — DB	O.E. cylftun. *Tun* (settlement) on a *scylf* (bank or ridge).
I9	East Langton	Langtone — DB	O.E. *langa tun* — a long settlement. East is the position in relation to the other Langtons.
G/H10	East Norton	Nortone — DB	*North tun* (settlement) north of another place.
***C/10**	Eastwell	Estuuelle — DB	Eastern *wella* (spring or stream).
C/10	Eaton	Aitona — 1127 — Leicestershire Survey	The *tun* (settlement) on land surrounded by water.
***E/11**	Edmondthorpe	Edmerestorp — DB	Eadmar's *thorp* (farm).
***H/4**	Elmesthorpe	Ailmerestorp 1207 — Curia Regis Rolls	AEthelmar's *thorp* (farm).
H6	Enderby	Andretesbie — DB	Eindrioi's *by* (village or homestead).
G7	Evington	Avintone — DB	The *tun* (settlement) of Eafa's people.
***D9**	Eye Kettleby	Chitebie — DB	Ketil's *by* (farm). The village is on a tributary of the river Eye.

*I5	Fenny Drayton	Draitone — DB	O.E. *drag* (a portage). Perhaps a place where boats are dragged over a narrow piece of land or past an obstruction in a river. Cox: place where hauling is necessary. The village is on heavy wet ground.
I7	Fleckney	Flechenie — DB	Flecca's well-watered land or Flecca's piece of dry ground in the fen.
I8/9	Foxton	Foxtone — DB	*Tun* (settlement) where foxes abounded.
D10	Freeby	Fredebi — DB	Fraeth's *by* (village or homestead).
G8/9	Frisby by Galby	Frisebi — DB	The Frisian's *by* (village or homestead).
I5	Frolesworth	Frellesworde — DB	Freothulf's *worth* (homestead).
E/F8	Gaddesby	Gadesbi — DB	Gadd's *by* (village or homestead).
G8	Galby	Galbi — DB	Possibly a noun: *gall* (sterile soil).
D11	Garthorpe	Garthorp 1125 — Leicestershire	Geiri's *thorp* (farm).
J6	Gilmorton	Mortone — DB	The original name was Morton. The *tun* (settlement) on the *moor.* Gil is O.E. *gylden* meaning literally golden. There must have been something splendid about the settlement for such a phrase to be coined.
H8	Glen Magna (Great)	Glen — DB Aet Glenne 849 Cartularium Saxonicum	Probably an old name of the river. Sence which may be the same as the British *glenno* meaning valley Welsh is *glyn.*
H6	Glen Parva	See Glen Magna	
GF/6	Glenfield	Clanefelds — DB	*Cleaen* (clean) *feld* (open country).
H/9	Glooston	Glorestone — DB	Glor's *tun* (settlement).
H9	Goadby	Goutebi — DB	Gauti's *by* (village or homestead).
H9	Goadby Marwood	Goutebi — DB	Gouti's *by* (village or homestead). Held in part by William Maureward in 1316.
*E5	Grace Dieu	la Gracedeu 1243 Episcopal Registers	God's grace. Gracedieu was a monastery.
*I9	Great Bowden	Bugedone — DB	Bucga's *dun* (hill). Bucga is a woman's name.
E9/10	Great Dalby	Dalbi — DB	*By* (village or settlement) in a *dael* (valley). Original name was Wold Dalby corrupted over the centuries to Old Dalby.

H/I11	Great Easton	Estone — DB	O.E. *east tun* — eastern tun (settlement).
GH/8	Great Stretton	Stratone — DB	*Tun* (settlement) on a Roman road.
D/8	Grimston	Grimestone — DB	Grimr's *tun* (settlement).
F5/6	Groby	Grobi — DB	Old Scan *grof* means a torrent and the gully formed by it, a pit or hollow. The *by* (village or settlement) at the pit. Half a mile away is a tarn.
I8	Gumley	Gutmundeslea — DB	Godmund's *leah* (glade, clearing, meadow).
H10	Hallaton	Alctone — DB	The *tun* (settlement) in a *halh* (narrow secluded valley, or a corner of land).
***G9**	Halstead	Elstede — DB	O.E. *heald* (a place of refuge or temporary abode). The meaning would be a place of shelter for cattle. Cox suggests that it might also mean a fortified place.
***F8**	Hamilton	Hamelton 1125 — Leicestershire Survey	Original form doubtful although it may be Hamela's *tun* (settlement).
C9	Harby	Hardebi — DB	Hjortr's *by* (village or settlement).
***B11**	Harston	Herstan — DB	O.E. *hara stan* — (grey stone) this could have been a boundary stone.
***D5**	Hathern	Avederne — DB	The hawthorn or the white thorn.
F3	Heather	Hadre — DB	*Heather* — this might mean a heath.
H3	Higham-on-the-Hill	Hecham 1220 — Episcopal Registers.	High *ham* (village or homestead).
***I/J5**	High Cross		Site of the Roman settlement of Venonae. This is where Watling Street and Fosse Way cross.
H/I4	Hinckley	Hinchelie — DB	Hynca's *leah* (woodland, glade).
D/E8	Hoby	Hobie — DB	The *by* (village or settlement) at the *hoh* (headland).
***D/9**	Holwell	Hollewelle — DB	*Wella* (stream) in a *holle* (deep valley).
***H/11**	Holyoak	Haliach — DB	Holy Oak.
H10	Horninghold	Horniwale — DB	The *wald* or woodland of the Horningas. Horninghold is in a winding valley and Horningas may be the dwellers in the *horna* (bend).
***C/9**	Hose	Hoches — DB	O.E. *hohas* or *hogas* plural of *hoh* — hill or spur of land.
D6	Hoton	Hohtone — DB	O.E. *hoh — tun.* The *tun* (settlement) on a *hoh* (spur of the hill).

G8	Houghton-on-the-Hill	Hohtone — DB	*Tun* (settlement) on a *hoh* (spur of the hill)
***E/4**	Hugglescote	Hukelescot — 1227 Charter Rolls	Hucel's *cot* (cottage(s)).
***G7**	Humberstone	Humerstane — DB	Hunbeorht's stone.
H5	Huncote	Hunecote — DB	Huna's *cot* (cottage(s)).
G/F8	Hungarton	Hungretone — DB	*Tun* (settlement) with poor soil where people had to starve.
J7	Husbands Bosworth	Baresworde — DB	Bar's *worth* (homestead). Husbandsmen's Bosworth i.e. rural (There is also Market Bosworth).
F4	Ibstock	Ibestoche — DB	Ibba's *stoc* (place) B.C. — Ibba's dairy farm.
H8/9	Ilston-on-the-Hill	Elvestone — DB	Iolf's *tun* (settlement).
FG/8	Ingarsby	Inuuaresbie — DB	Ingvar's *by* (village or homestead).
C/D4	Isley Walton	Walton 1120—1135 Episcopal Registers	*Tun* (settlement) in a *wald* (wood).
C5	Kegworth	Cacheuuorde — DB	Ek. finds the meaning obscure but B.C. is happy about Caegga's wood.
FG/8	Keyham	Caiham — DB	Caega's *ham* (village or homestead). B.C. thinks that it could be *ham* on gravel soil.
***H/10**	Keythorpe	Caitorp — DB	Caega's *thorp* (farmstead).
I8	Kibworth Beauchamp	Chiburde — DB	Cybba's *worth* (homestead). Held by Walter de Bellocampo c. 1125 Leicestershire Survey.
J8	Kibworth Harcourt	See Beauchamp	Held by Robert de Herewecurt in 1202. Harcourt from Harcourt in Normandy.
H7	Kilby	Cilebi — DB	O.E. *cildatun* — the *tun* (settlement) of the youth of noble birth.
J7	Kimcote	Chenemundescote — DB	Cynemund's *cot* (cottage(s)).
GH8	Kings Norton	Nortone — DB	North *tun* — the *tun* (settlement) north of another. This village was part of the royal desmesne.
***E/9**	Kirby Bellars	Chirchebi — DB	Village with a church. Beler is a nickname from the french — *belier* — ram.
G5/7	Kirby Muxloe	Carbi — DB	Kaerir's *by* (village or homestead). Muxloe is a local surname.
GI7	Knaptoft	Chapetot — DB	O.E. *cnapa* boy or young man (or even servant or meniel) *toft* (homestead).

*G7	Knighton	Cnihtetone – DB	O.E. *cnihta tun*. The *tun* (settlement) of the knights or the retainers. Knights and retainers would have had the same meaning in the pre-conquest period.
*B/10	Knipton	Cnipetone – DB	*Knip* (narrow place). Knipton is in a narrow valley with high hills at its sides. B.C. – The *tun* (settlement) beneath the steep hillside.
F10	Knossington	Nossitone – DB	O.E. *cnoss hill* (rounded hill), *tun* (settlement).
I/J8	Laughton	Lachestone – DB	O.E. The *tun* (settlement) where the *leac* (leek(s)) are grown.
G10	Launde	Landa 1163	The open space in the woodland.
G6/7	Leicester	Legorensis Civitas 803 – Cartularium Saxonicum. Ledecestre – DB	This is probably the *caester* of the dwellers on the Legra. It has been suggested that Legra was an alternative name for the Soar, but that is not likely as the name Soar is of British origin. The name Legra survives in Leire which stands on a tributary of the Soar.
I5/6	Leire	Legre – DB	Very likely an old river name. See Leicester.
*H/3	Lindley	Lindle – 1209–35 Episcopal Registers	O.E. The *leah* (glade, clearing, meadow) where the *lin* (flax) was grown.
J9	Little Bowden	See Great Bowden	
E9/10	Little Dalby	See Great Dalby	
GH/8	Little Stretton	See Great Stretton	
*H6	Littlethorpe	Torp – DB	The *thorp* (farmstead) later the little *thorp*.
C4/5	Lockington	Lochamtona – 971 Codex Diplomaticus Aevi Saxonici	O.E. *loc ham tun.* The *tun* (settlement) of the people by the *loc ham* (homestead, enclosure).
G10	Loddington	Ludintine – DB	The *tun* (settlement) of Luda's people.
B/C9	Long Clawson	Clachestone – DB	Clac's *tun* (settlement). Long village.
D4/5	Long Whatton	Wacthon – 1125 – Leicestershire Survey	O.E. *hweate* (wheat) *tun* (settlement). B.C. suggests that this might be Wacca's *tun* (settlement).
D5/6	Loughborough	Lucteburne – DB	Luhhede's *burg* (fortified place).
F9	Lowesby	Glowesbi – DB	Lausi's *by* (village or homestead).
G5/6	Lubbesthorpe	Lupestorp – DB	Lubb's *thorp* (farmstead).

J8/9	Lubenham	Lubanham — DB	Lubba's *ham* (homestead, enclosure).
J5/6	Lutterworth	Lutresurde — DB	The first element may be a river name — Hlutre derived from O.E. *hluttor* meaning clean, pure. If so Hlutre was an old name of the Swift.
F9	Marefield	Merdefelde — DB	*Feld* (open country) frequented by martins O.E.
G3/4	Market Bosworth	Boseworde — DB	Bosa's *worth* (homestead).
I/J9	Market Harborough	Hauerberga 1177 — Pipe Rolls	O.E. *haefera* (oats). Hill where oats were grown.
F4/5	Markfield	Merchenfeld — DB	The *feld* (open land &/or country) of the Mercians.
E/F2	Measham	Messeham — DB	*Ham* (homestead or enclosure) on River Mease.
I10	Medbourne	Medbourne — DB	O.E. *Maed* (meadow) *burna* (stream). Stream with meadows on its banks.
D/E9	Melton Mowbray	Medeltone — DB	O.E. The *middle tun* (settlement). Held by Roger de Moubray c. 1125, Leicestershire Survey. Mowbray from Montbray in Normandy.
J6	Misterton	Minstretone — DB	The *tun* (settlement) of the monastery. Or the *tun* with a church.
E6	Mountsorrel	Munt Sorel — 1152 Charters and Rolls in the British Museum	The place had a strong Norman castle whose name may be a transplantation of Montsoreau near Saumur or Mont Sorel near Rennes. B.C. suggests that the meaning is sorrel-coloured hill.
I/J7	Mowsley	Muselai — DB	Mouse-infested *leah* (glade, clearing, meadow).
***A/10**	Muston	Moston — 1125 Leicestershire Registers	O.E. *mus* (mouse) *tun* (settlement) — probably a mouse infested site.
H6	Narborough	Norburg — DB	*North burg* (fortified place).
***C/8**	Nether Broughton	Broctone — DB	O.E. *broc tun*. The *tun* (settlement) on a brook.
I10	Nevill Holt	Holt 1166 -- The Red Book of the Exchequer.	*Holt* (wood). Robert de Nevill was patron of Nevill Holt in 1120—35 — Episcopal Registers.
G4	Newbold Verdon	Newebold — DB	New building. Came to Bertram de Verdon. The name is from Verdun in France.
***H/7**	Newton Harcourt	Niwetone — DB	New *tun* (settlement). Burgoland from the Birgilon family. The name means Burgundian.

F5/6	Newtown Linford	Newton 1325 Inquisitiones Post Mortem	New *tun* (settlement) at the ford where the *lind* (lime trees) grow.
***E/83**	Normanton-le-Heath	Normenton – 1209–35 Episcopal Registers	The *tun* (settlement) of the north-men or Norwegians.
J7	North Kilworth	Chiveleswordе – DB	The *worth* (homestead) of Cyfel's people.
***F/2**	Norton juxta Twycross	Nortone – DB	*North tun* (settlement) north of another.
H9	Nosely	Noveslei – DB	Nothwulf's *leah* (glade, clearing, meadow).
G/H7	Oadby	Oldebi – DB	Audi's *by* (village or homestead).
G3	Odstone	Odestone – DB	Odd's *tun* (settlement).
E9/10	Old Dalby	Dalbi – DB	The *by* (village or homestead) in a *dael* (a valley). Old Dalby is actually *wold*. Dalby on the wold.
***F2**	Orton-on-the-Hill	Wortone – DB	*Ufera* (upper) *tun* (settlement).
G4	Osbaston	Sbernestun – DB	Osbeorn's *tun* (settlement).
D4	Osgathorpe	Osgodtorp – DB	Asgot's *thorp* (farmstead).
F9/10	Owston	Osulvestone – DB	Oswulf's *tun* (settlement).
E3	Packington	Pachintone – DB Packinton 1043 – Diplomatarium Anglicum.	Paeca's *tun* (settlement).
I7	Peatling Magna	Petlinge – DB	Peotla's people.
I6/7	Peatling Parva	See Peatling Magna	
H4/5	Peckleton	Pechintone – DB	Pechtla's *tun* (settlement).
***F10**	Pickwell	Pichewell – DB	*Pick* (peak) *wella* (stream), stream or spring by the peaks. The place is near two high hills.
***A10**	Plungar	Plungar c. 1125 – Leicestershire Survey	O.E. *plum gara* – a point of land where plum trees grew.
H5	Potters Marston	Mersitone – DB Potteresmerston 1043	*Tun* (settlement) by a marsh. There must have been potteries here.
D6	Prestwold	Prestewolde – DB	The priest's *wudu* (wood).
***F9**	Quenby	Qveneberie – DB	O.E. *cwene burg.* The queen's manor. The second element *by* added later.
F7/8	Queniborough	Cuinburg – DB	O.E. *cwene burg* the queen's manor.
E6	Quorndon or Quorn	Querendon 1209–35 Episcopal Registers	O.E. *cweorndun* – *dun* (hill) where the mill-stones (quern-stones) were got.

***D8**	Ragdale	Ragendele – DB	*Dael* (valley) with narrow track going through it (B.C.). Ek. considered this interpretation but was not sure of it.
GS	Ratby	Rotabie – DB	Rota's *by* (village or homestead). This might well be the Rota whose name is preserved in Rutland.
***G2**	Ratcliffe Culey	Redeclive – DB	O.E. *reade clif* (red bank or cliff). Held by Hugo de Culy in 1285. Culey from Culey in Normandy.
E7	Ratcliffe-on-the-Wreake	Radeclive – DB	O.E. *reade clif* (red cliff). B.C. 'A marl cliff'.
E3	Ravenstone	Ravenstun – DB	Hrafn's *tun* (settlement).
E7/8	Rearsby	Redresbi – DB	Reidarr's *by* (village or homestead).
B10	Redmile	Redmelde – DB	Place with red soil. B.C. thinks that it is the *thorp* (farmstead) belonging to Redmile.
G/H9	Rolleston	Rovestone – DB	Hrolf's *tun* (settlement).
D/E8	Rotherby	Redebi – DB	Hreidar's *by* (settlement).
E/F6	Rothley	Rodolei – DB	O.E. *roth* (clearing) *leah* (glade, clearing, meadow) Woodland glade.
I7/8	Saddington	Sadintone – DB	The *tun* (settlement) of etymology obscure.
***C11**	Saltby	Saltebi – DB	Salte's *by* (village or homestead).
I5	Sapcote	Scepecote – DB	O.E. *sceap* (sheep) *cot* (shelter).
***D10**	Saxby	Saxebi – DB	Saxi's *by* (village or homestead).
***D8**	Saxelby	Saxelbie – DB	Saxulf's *by* (village or homestead).
DG/10	Scalford	Scaldeford – DB	O.E. *scald* (the shallow ford).
G8	Scraptoft	Scrapentot – DB	Skrapi's *toft* (homestead).
D11	Seagrave	Satgrave – DB	O.E. *set* (ford or pit or pool) *graf* (ditch).
***D11**	Sewstern	Sewesten – DB	Etymology obscure. The first element may be O.E. Seofon (seven).
F/G3	Shakerstone	Sacrestone – DB	O.E. *sceacers* (robber). The *tun* (settlement) of the robbers.
H9	Shangton	Santone – DB	O.E. *scanca* (shank, leg). The word is used here in the sense of a long narrow spur of a hill. The *tun* (settlement) at the spur of the hill.
I5	Sharnford	Scerneforde – DB	The O.E. *scearn* (muddy) ford.

K6	Shawell	Sawelle – DB	O.E. *sceap* (boundary) *wella* (stream).
I7	Shearsby	Svevesbi – DB	Skeifr's *by* (village or homestead).
G2/3	Sheepy Magna	Scepehe – DB	O.E. *sceapea* (sheep river or island). Piece of dry land in a fen, where sheep could graze.
G2/3	Sheepy Parva	See Sheepy Magna	
*H3	Shenton	Scenctun – DB	*Tun* (settlement) on River Sence.
D/E5	Shepshed	Scepeshefde – DB	*Sceap* (sheep) *heaford* (head, or hill) – hill where the sheep grazed.
*H3	Sibson	Sibetesdone – DB	Sigebed's *dun* (hill).
E7	Sileby	Siglesbie – DB	Sigulfr's *by* (village or homestead).
G9	Skeffington	Sciftitone – DB	The *tun* (settlement) of Sceaft's people.
H/J10	Slawston	Slagestone – DB	Slag's *tun* (settlement).
I8	Smeeton Westerby	Westerbi – DB	*Smeeton* – smith's *tun* – the enclosure or settlement of the smiths. Westerby – the westerly *by* (village or homestead).
F2/3	Snareston	Snarchetone – DB	Snar's *tun* (settlement).
E3	Snibston	Suipestona – c. 1125 Leicestershire Survey	Snip's *tun* (settlement).
F9/10	Somerby	Sumerlidebie – DB	Sumarlidi's *by* (village or homestead). This personal name means 'summer warrior'.
F8	South Croxton	Crochestone – DB	Croc's *tun* (settlement).
K6	South Kilworth	Chivelesworde – DB	The *worth* (homestead) of Cyfel's people.
C11	Sproxton	Sprotone – DB	Sprok's *tun* (settlement).
E4	Stanton-under-Bardon	Stantone – DB	The *tun* (settlement) on stoney ground on the slope of Bardon Hill. B.C. thinks that possibly this means a hill with barrows on it.
*D10	Stapleford	Stapeford – DB	O.E. *stapolford* – ford marked by a *stapol* (post).
*H4	Stapleton	Stapletone – DB	The *tun* (settlement) by a *stapol* (post). The exact meaning is not clear.
B9/10	Stathern	Stachedirne – DB	*'Stake thorn'.* Possible O.E. 'boundary post' or 'boundary thorn'.

D3	Staunton Harold	Stantone – DB	*Tun* (settlement) on stoney ground. Held by Harold de Leec in the 12th. Century.
H10/ 11	Stockerston	Stoctone – DB	O.E. *stocc faesten* (stronghold built of tree-trunks).
***H3**	Stoke Golding	Stokes – 1200 Curia Regis Rolls	O.E. *stock* (place). B.C. says that this was originally a dairy farm. Held by Petrus de Goldinton in 1200.
***C/10**	Stonesby	Stovenebi – DB	Stofn's *by* (village or homestead).
H/I5	Stoney Stanton	Stantone – DB	The *tun* (settlement) on stoney ground.
H/I9	Stonton Wyville	Stantone – DB	Either the *tun* (settlement) on stoney ground; or the stone-built *tun* (settlement). The manor was held by Robert de Wivill in 1209. The name comes from Gouville in Normandy.
G7/8	Stoughton	Stoctone – DB	O.E. *stoc* (place) *tun* (settlement).
F2	Stretton-en-le-Field	Stretone – DB	The *tun* (settlement) on a Roman road. Most strettons are on Roman roads.
H3/4	Sutton Cheney	Sutone – DB	O.E. *suth tun* – southern settlement. Family name of Cheney from one of the places of that name in France.
***I5**	Sutton-in-the-Elms	Sutone – DB	The south *tun* (settlement).
E4	Swannington	Sueniton – DB	Sweppi's *tun* (settlement).
F6	Swithland	Swithellund – DB	O.Scan *lundr* (grove) and *switha* (burnt). Perhaps a grove cleared by burning.
***D9**	Sysonby	Sistenebi – DB	Sigstein's *by* (village or homestead).
F7	Syston	Sitestone – DB	Sigehaes' *tun* (settlement).
J8	Theddingworth	Tediworde – DB	The *worth* (homestead) of Peoda's people.
***F4**	Thornton	Torrenton – 1209–1235 Leicestershire Survey	The *tun* (settlement) where the thorn bushes grew.
***D9**	Thorpe Arnold	Torp – DB	*Thorp* (outlying farmstead). The place was called Thorp Ernad in the Episcopal Registers of 1239: but there is no explanation of the name.
I9	Thorp Langton	Torp – DB	*Thorp* (outlying farmstead) near Langton.
***D9**	Thorpe Satchville	Thorp – 1125 – Leicestershire Survey	*Thorp* (outlying farmstead). Held by Radulfus de Secheville in 1210. The name is from Secqueville in Normandy.

***E9**	Thringstone	Trangesbi — DB	Traeingr's *tun* (settlement). Second element originally *by* (village or homestead).
F6	Thurcaston	Turchitelestone — DB	Thorketil's *tun* (settlement).
H5	Thurlaston	Turlaeuestona — 1166 — Pipe Rolls	Thorleif's *tun* (settlement).
E7/8	Thrussington	Turstanstone — DB	Thorstein's *tun* (settlement).
F7	Thurmaston	Turmodestone — DB	Thormoth's *tun* (settlement).
G8	Thurnby	Turnebi — DB	Thyrne's *by* (village or homestead).
G9	Tilton-on-the-Hill	Tillintone	Tila's *tun* (settlement).
G/H9	Tugby	Tochebi — DB	Toki's *by* (village or homestead).
H8/9	Tur Langton	Terlintone — DB	The *tun* (settlement) of Tyrhyel's people.
F/G2	Twycross	Tvicros — DB	B.C. thinks that this is probably a place which possessed two carved crosses. Unlikley to be a double cross sign showing the way at a crossroads, which is Ekwalls suggestion.
F9	Twyford	Tuiuorde — DB	Double ford; either one over a river that had two arms or perhaps a place where there were two fords side by side.
J5	Ullesthorpe	Ulestorp — DB	Ulf's *thorp* (outlying farmstead).
E5	Ulverscroft	Ulvescroft 1174 — Charters and Rolls in British Museum	Ulf's *croft* (enclosure).
J6	Walcote	Walecote — DB	The *cot* or cottages of the *walh* (British) serfs.
C/D10	Waltham-on-the-Wolds	Waltham — DB	O.E. *ham* (village or homestead) at the *wald* (wood).
J7	Walton	Waltone — DB	The *tun* (settlement) of the British serfs.
D7	Walton-on-the-Wolds	Waleton — DB	The *tun* (settlement) of the Britons or the (British) serfs.
F6/7	Wanlip	Anlepe — DB	O.E. *anliepe* (isolated, single). The place was a swamp and the name might have referred to a narrow footbridge or some stepping stones which could only be crossed in single file.
***D9**	Wartnaby	Worcnodebie — DB	Waercnod's *by* (village or homestead).

C19	Welham	Waledeham — DB	Weol's *ham* (village or homestead) B.C. Ek. the *ham* by the *wella* (river). The Welland.
C19	West Langton	Langestone — DB	Long *tun* (settlement).
G10	Whatborough	Wetberge — DB	O.E. *hweate* (wheat), *beorg* (hill).
C16	Whetstone	Westham — DB	This name may refer to an ancient standing stone.
*E4	Whitwick	Witewic — DB	Either Hwita's *wic* or white *wic* (dairy farm).
H7	Wigston Magna	Wichingestone — DB	Viking's *tun* (settlement).
C14/9	Wigston Parva	Wicestan — DB	Possibly Wicga's stone. The southern boundary of the village is Watling Street and the village is about half a mile from Venonae at High Cross. The stone referred to might well be a Roman milestone or similar.
C16	Willoughby Waterless	Wilebi — DB	The *by* (village or homestead) among the willows and then, later, water meadows.
H7	Wistow	Wistanestov — DB	Wigstan's *sot* or holy place.
G10	Withcote	Wicoc — DB	O.E. *withis* — (willow) and *cocc* — (heap) here meaning a clump of willows.
H2/3	Witherley	Witheredel — DB	Wigthryth's *leah* (glade, clearing or meadow). This is a woman's name.
E5/6	Woodhouse	Wodehuses — 1209—1235 Episcopal Registers.	The houses in a wood.
	Woodhouse Eaves	See Woodhouse	
D3/4	Worthington	Wereitone — DB	The *tun* (settlement) of the Wurthingas.
D9	Wyfordby	Wivordebies — DB	O.E. *ford* by a *wig* (a temple).
D7	Wymeswold	Wimundewal — DB	Wigmund's *wald* (wood).
D/E11	Wymondham	Wimundesham — DB	Wigmund's *ham* (village or homestead).

Rutland

E11	Ashwell	Exewelle — DB	*Ash wella* (stream or spring).
G11	Ayston	Aethelstanestun — 1046 Codex Diplomaticus Aevi Saxonici.	Aethelstan's *tun* (settlement).

F11	Barleythorpe	Bolaresthorp — 1203 Feet of Fines	*Thorp* (the outlying farmstead). John le Bolar is mentioned in connection with Oakham in 1200. Later the name became 'barley growing *thorp'*.
***F12**	Barnsdale	Bernardeshull — 1202 Assize Rolls.	Beornheard's Hill.
***E11**	Barrow	Berghes — 1206 Curia Regis Rolls	O.E. *beorg* (hill or mound).
G12/ 13	Barrowden	Berchedone — DB	O.E. beorgadun — *dun* (hill) with barrow or burial mounds.
G/10	Belton	Bealton — 1167 Pipe Rolls	Ekwall thinks that bel might be O.N. *bil* — interval, interspace. If so the word might have been used of a glade in a forest or a piece of dry land in fenny country. B.C. interprets the name as '*tun* on open ground in a forest or *tun* on dry land surrounded by bog.'
G/11/ 12	Bisbrooke	Bitlesbroch — DB	Bitel's *broc* (brook or stream).
F10/ 11	Braunston	Branteston — 1167 Pipe Rolls	Brant's *tun* (settlement).
G/11	Brooke	Broc — 1176 Pipe Rolls	O.E. *broc* (the brook). The Gwash.
F11/ 12	Burley	Burgelea — DB	*Leah* (woodland glade) or clearing by or belonging to a *burgh* (fortified place).
H/I11	Caldecott	Caldecot — 1246 Charter Rolls	O.E. *calde* (cold) *cot* (shelter or hut). This may refer to a hut or shelter for animals or wayfarers in an exposed position.
E13	Clipsham	Kilpesham — 1203 Curia Regis Rolls.	Cylp's *ham* (village or homestead).
E12	Cottesmore	Cotesmore — DB	Cott's *mor* (moor or wasteland).
G12/ 13	Edith Weston	Westona — 1167 Pipe Rolls	O.E. *west tun* — western tun (settlement) a *tun* west of another. Edith from Queen Edith, wife of Edward the Confessor, who had possessions in Rutland at the time of the Norman conquest.
F11	Egleton	Egiltun — 1209 Forest Charters	Ecgwulf's *tun* (settlement).
F12/ 13	Empingham	Epingeham — DB	The *ham* (village or homestead) of Empa's people.
E14	Essendine	Esindone — DB	Esa's *denu* (valley).
F12	Exton	Exentune — DB	O.E. *exna* (oxen) *tun* (settlement) probably means ox farm.

G/H/ 12	Glaston	Gladestone — DB	Glathr's *tun* (settlement).
F13	Great Casterton	Castretone — DB	*Tun* (settlement) by a Roman fort. There are remains of a camp at Casterton. Ermine Street crosses the River Gwash here.
E12/ 13	Greetham	Gretham — DB	O.E. *greot* — gravel. The *ham* (village or homestead) on gravel.
G11	Gunthorpe	Gunetorp — 1200 Curia Regis Rolls	Gunni's *thorp* (outlying farmstead).
F12	Hambleton	Hameldun — DB	Village situated near a hill. O.E. *hamol* means 'maimed'. This may mean bare treeless or cut-off (level).
G13	Ketton	Chetene — DB	An old name of the River Chater. Second element is O.E. *ea* (river). *Tun* (settlement).
F11	Langham	Langham — 1202 Assize Rolls	Long *ham* (village or homestead).
H11	Lyddington	Lidentone — DB	*Tun* (settlement) on River Hylde. O.E. *hylde* (a noisy stream).
F13	Little Casterton	See Great Casterton	
G12	Lyndon	Lindon — 1167 — Pipe Rolls	*Lind* (Lime-tree) *dun* (hill).
G11/ 12	Manton	Manatone — 1130 — Documents preserved in France	Manna's (possibly personal name or *manan* meaning common or communually owned) *tun* (settlement).
E11/ 12	Market Overton	Overtune — DB	O.E. *ufera tun* the settlement on a slope or ridge. This place was known for its market as early as the 12th century.
G12	Morcott	Morcote — DB	*Cot* (cottage or hut) on the *moor* (moor or wasteland).
F/ G12	Normanton	Normantona — 1209 Episcopal Registers	The *tun* (settlement) of the north-men or Norwegians.
G12/ 13	North Luffenham	Lufenham — DB	Luffa's *ham* (village or homestead).
F11	Oakham	Ocheham — DB	Occa's *ham* (village or homestead).
E13	Pickworth	Pikesworth — 1203 — Assize Rolls	Pica's *worth* (homestead).
G12	Pilton	Pilton — 1202 — Assize Rolls	O.E. *pyll* — a pool in a river. The *tun* (settlement) by a *pyll* or creek. This must mean the Chater.
G11	Preston	Prestetona — 1130 Pipe Rolls	O.E. *preosta* (priests) *tun* (settlement).

G11	Ridlington	Redlinctune – DB	Hrethel's *tun* (settlement).
E/ F14	Ryhall	Riehale – DB	A *halh* (a corner, angle) where rye was grown. This could mean the bend in the River Gwash.
H12	Seaton	Seieton – DB	First element could be the name of a brook – *seage* (trickling or slow-moving). Both Ek. and B.C. think that this is probably a personal name Seaga's *tun* (settlement).
G12/ 13	South Luffenham	See North Luffenham	
H11	Stoke Dry	Stoch – DB	O.E. *stoc* – a place (the dairy farm) The village is on a hill above the valley of the Eye Brook.
E12/ 13	Stretton	Stratone – DB	*Tun* (settlement) on a Roman Road. This place is on Ermine Street.
E11	Teigh	Tie – DB	O.E. *teag* (enclosure).
E12	Thistleton	Tistetune – DB	*Tun* (settlement) where the *thistel* (thistles) abound. Thistles grow on the sites of deserted buildings. There is a Roman-British site half a mile S.W. of the village.
F13	Tickencote	Tichecote – DB	*Cot* (shelter) for *ticcen* (young goats).
F13	Tinwell	Tidinwelle – DB	This is obscure but could mean the *wella* (stream or well) of Tida's people.
G13	Tixover	Tochesovre – DB	O.E. *ofer* (bank or slope) for *ticcen* (young goats).
H11	Uppingham	Yppingeham – 1067 British Museum Charters	1st element O.E. *Yppingas or Uppingas* (people on the hill). *ham* (village or homestead).
G/ H11	Wardley	Werlea – 1067 – British Museum	O.E. *weard* – (watch,) *leah* – (open place in a wood.) Wardley stands on a hill above the Eye Brook, this would have made a good look-out.
E10/ 11	Whissendine	Wichingedene – DB	O.E. *denu* (valley) of the Wicingas.
F12	Whitwell	Witewelle – DB	*Hwit* (White) (spring or stream). There is a *wella* small stream here.
G12	Wing	Wengeford – 1046 Codex Diplomaticus Aevi Saxonici.	O.N. *vengi* (field or garden).